THE GREATEST
WITCH
I EVER MET

THE GREATEST WITCH I EVER MET

DENNIS MEADOWS

The Greatest Witch I Ever Met
Copyright © 2020 by Dennis Meadows. All rights reserved.

No part of this publication may be reproduced, stored in a retrieval system or transmitted in any way by any means, electronic, mechanical, photocopy, recording or otherwise without the prior permission of the author except as provided by USA copyright law.

The opinions expressed by the author are not necessarily those of URLink Print and Media.

1603 Capitol Ave., Suite 310 Cheyenne, Wyoming USA 82001
1-888-980-6523 | admin@urlinkpublishing.com

URLink Print and Media is committed to excellence in the publishing industry.

Book design copyright © 2020 by URLink Print and Media. All rights reserved.

Published in the United States of America

ISBN 978-1-64753-289-5 (Paperback)
ISBN 978-1-64753-290-1 (Digital)

05.03.20

Contents

Chapter 1: Witches 7
Chapter 2 9
Chapter 3 11
Chapter 4 15
Chapter 5 19
Chapter 6 23
Chapter 7: Amendment #2 27
Chapter 8: Chickens Come Home 31
Chapter 9: Vacation Time 35
Chapter 10: Lunch Time 37

About the Author 43
About the Book 45

CHAPTER 1
Witches

This book is about people of whom I have met. It will help people to know the truth. It will help us to understand the KJV Bible.

As we start with Exodus 22:18, no witch is to live. I am using the KJV version. In Deuteronomy 18:10-12, we learn no witch was to live. In Leviticus 20:27, a witch was stoned to death.

The KJV version bible is the best ever produced. The world has many bibles, but the KJV is the only true bible of its kind. We all know the others have been perverted. It is why the true church has fallen away. It is also why the church has as many witches in it as on the outside.

As we go on, I believe that the public schools have many witches in them. When I was in eighth grade, I learned more about them. It seemed a few of the teachers tried to teach evolution. They tried to ram it down our throats. They would curse a lot and even slap some in the face if they didn't go along with them. One science teacher tried to make us believe that we would turn into a frog, or something, after we died. One place I worked at had many witches in it. It seemed many of the people were lost, and some just not right with God. A few were in cults at one time or another. Even today I believe that some of the churches have turned into a cult like place. They use three or four bibles, and many of the people are from the yuppie crowd. They have always had plenty and want more. Yes, one witch that I met looked like a true Christian because she wore long dresses that fooled a lot of people. I sort of liked her myself until I found out that when she was fifteen, she had gone crazy and never got over it, and I believe that part. I was not sure if she was really saved.

CHAPTER 2

Witches are made up of people. I have met many of whom I will call a witch. One of whom was after money and ,of course, many are like that. One called me about 8:00 and wanted me to supposedly buy real estate. It was a scam. She was just a street walker that worked for a company from another state. Then the witch that couldn't get a raise and was going to try to sue the owner for not paying her more. She tried to get me to give her $500 for a quick fling, but of course I didn't go for it. She even went to a Baptist Church, but was most likely not saved. She got a job about thirty miles away for $2.00

more an hour. Then I remember one witch and ,of course, she was a young street walker. She had come from another land. She had told me her problems and how she was in a big city in the northeast. She had told me that she was from man to man. To be honest, I really felt sorry for her. She must have felt bad about it, because she was wanting money from me that I didn't have. She had a new hippie from a big city. They were about as wicked as they came.

One time I met a witch, and she was a school teacher, and I know several teachers, and we would have dinner once in a while. She said that she was saved, but I do not know. She did not dress much like a real lady, only when she went to church. I guess many do that these days. One time, she wanted me to get her a couple of certain movies for her, and I did. That evening after dinner we started watching them, but I had to pull the first one because it was too bad. She had plans for me from the words she told me, but it wasn't God's plan. She was very covetous.

CHAPTER 3

At one church that I attended they did fairly well, until they voted in a new preacher. Many churches do that every few years. It seems he started out well, but one was about like Solomon. He preached fairly well for a couple of years. Then he started using different Bibles. He was running off anyone who didn't go along with his Bibles. Many people left. I guess hundreds. The music changed. I guess they fired the music leaders. We went from good Godly music to the new worldly music.

I remember the so-called preacher, of course, it is the new name used for those that do not preach the true Bible. One of the members that was there was in jail I guess at one time, and the so-called preacher would bring it up in his sermon about every week or two. As most of us know that know the Bible, is that all of our righteousness are as filthy rags. I know several preachers that were in jail. Paul the great missionary was there plenty of times. Peter was there. Yes, I remember where that man and his wife sat. The church I was going to was like the church of Laodicea. It is in Revelation 4:14-22.

It wasn't long before I found out that many churches have turned away from their first love. The one church that had a so-called preacher from the church on Seven Hills, he said he and his wife had gotten saved. He said he wanted to be a preacher, but the real reason was because he was sort of like Ahab in the Bible. He was after the dollar. Preachers are to be called, but as most of us know, many are after the dollar. I really wasn't a member of that church anymore, but I did go there sometimes. The church had become almost as a full-blown cult. One night, a lady told me that some, or perhaps, many of the people hated me in other words. I already knew that because they hated many other people that used to go there. They hated Jesus, and if he were here now, they would crucify him again. I thought they would hang me and still may, who knows? That church was like many others today. They are rich, and think they have need of nothing. One evening that I had gone to that big, rich, elite church, they had a business meeting. They were making plans for everyone to have background checks, and they were already doing it on many people, which is against the law. And most of us know, a background check many times is anything someone says about you, or me, or anyone. The so-called preacher from the church on Seven Hills gave me a dirty look, and didn't say hardly anything that night. He was one of the yuppie witches.

Chapter 4

One church that I had gone to had a traveling evangelist in it. I had done work for him and the office that they used. He had several children and used them to help raise money, and they would take big vacations during the summer and go overseas and islands and beg people at churches for money. One day, when I was working on their office, he and his son came over and were laughing at me and making fun of me for working. As we all know, Paul says to use our hands for work. They were like Ahab. The same man's wife said some perverted things to me.

She sang in the choir and put her hair up like a mushroom.

I remember one witch that I had worked for years ago. He made about one hundred and thirty thousand, and he and his wife, together with their three children, could not live on it. He had gotten hooked on drugs and even had his children on them, and told me he was going to get his wife on them. He only worked for the wealthy people. He did work for the city, and the county, and a judge friend of his who decided who would do the work no matter how high the price was. The witch had made more in two weeks than many people make in a year.

Then one of the so-called preachers at one of the churches of whom was a slender so-called man, would call me and want to know who I was going out with at the time. It was really none of his business. He was always running down people who were in churches that were as good as he was in. I remember his dad's look on his face one evening, and he was afraid. He should have been since his son was going around and breaking laws. The perverted man rides around town on a bike in the nighttime looking through windows, or to see his perverted friends. I guess I caught him early one morning going to see a man. This so-called preacher is supposed to have his doctor's degree.

The greatest mistake this person did was when he came to my house. He was peeping through the windows, doors, and taking pictures, I guess. Then I caught him red-handed, and his face turned white when I asked him why he was out there. He said that he was driving down the road and had a few minutes, and decided to park there. He started dancing around the vehicle he had bought it for. In other words, he had stolen it. He did it with the money from the church from the poor people. He makes more than $100,000 a year. The man with a doctorate had called me once about some woman that I had dinner with, months before. She may have been lost. She was full of envy. She heard a radio program that I was on and she had a hissy fit. I remember she said that I could not ever write books, or in other words, do anything for God. Well maybe she should read this book. She was twice my size and not even nice. I hope you can guess where she worked. I had done advertising there long before she ever worked there.

The woman was sort of like the one where the grandma wanted to get money. Her granddaughter had a hippie boyfriend and was wanting everything now. They were playing politics. The grandma tried to get me to say I said something bad when I didn't. She talked to the prosecutor, and he was a witch himself.

He told her that he would try to prosecute me if she would pay him enough money. Her husband told me that, too. They didn't want to spend $100,000 or more and then lose.

The witches have already lost. It is people like that who are running the country. It is not just people on the left either. I want you to relax and guess where that prosecutor is now. It would almost blow your mind if I told you.

Chapter 5

It seems that witches are everywhere. If you are truly saved, they want to destroy you. The one church that turned into a cult had a big parking lot and one of the last times that I was there, one of the cult leader's sons gave me a very proud look, like the Pharisee. It was like the woman that gave me a very proud look in the church one evening. It was less than two weeks, and God removed her forever.

Yes, one of the witches that was in a painting business didn't pay me all of the money. He was lost and a hippie, of course, and was in very deep sin. Also, the one that didn't pay me, who had sold car parts and hubcaps at different places, he didn't pay me for all the work I did for him. He was an usher at the door of a church. He is a lying witch. I remember one that was in real estate. He took my phone. I finally got it back. He got me for a few hundred. His wife wanted me to do bad things with her, but I didn't. Yes, the handyman witch that got me for a few hundred. The pictures say a lot. The so-called preacher with a big nose. I used to talk to him outside the cult church. Well, my dad lived to be about 75. His health was going down, so God took him home. Yes, this cult leader had the nerve to say that my dad died young, and yet his dad died at 64. I think that is the problem with the world. Some people get a piece of paper that says, in other words, that they are smarter than anyone else when I think many times, they are dumber.

It seems some people think they know it all. The so-called preacher that drove a bus came over to me one day in church while I was reading my Bible, and started screaming at me like a 2-year-old. His wife helped him get his doctor's degree, which only gave him more money. He came from one perverted church to another. He couldn't even preach and a lot of people left. I remember him putting his hands on my jacket and that is when I stood up. I think he thought I had a gun, but I didn't. I remember that in the early churches in every land, and ours, of course, the preachers all had a gun in case gangsters came in. Most all of the adults and people that came to church when our country got started carried a gun without a permit. I think I will listen to what the Bible says, not man's law. He is one of the typical Pharisees in the churches today.

Yes, the head witch of the cult had a big nose. It was about the time I stopped going to the cult that he was dancing around the pulpit. Most people would think they were at a wild concert. I think he thought I had a gun and was going to shoot him. He should have known that I was good with one since my phone was tapped because of people like him.

It wasn't long before that he was bragging how good he was at hunting. Really, he doesn't have a clue. The one deacon that used to call me was very afraid the last time I saw him and his wife at the cult church. He thought that I was going to hurt him very badly, but I didn't. He and others were breaking laws, and not only man's laws. He had told me to call him one time after church, and I did and he said perverted things to me. He was supposed to be the deacon over me, yet I never thought he was truly saved. It seems he wasn't right with God. He breaks laws all the time and pays his way out of it. He doesn't pay his help hardly anything to live on. He was chastised by God once, I know. All I can say is everyone should be invited, because Jesus invites everyone.

CHAPTER 6

Yes, and we all know that God is judging our land because of the bloodshed. People are shooting people even in churches, and I don't believe that they all go to heaven, because of the words of Jesus in John 14:6. People want to do away with history and the Bible.

One of the witches that goes around the country is a money guru. Some people call him the "money man". He goes around churches and says he tries to help people with their money. Well, I remember Jesus used gold as an example. Well, this yuppie, of course, was saying on the radio that he had heard, at one of the churches, of a business computer that had porn on it. The yuppie money man was bragging that all of his computers were of course, clean as a whistle.

The yuppie money man should not boast because guess who was on the tube showing off herself, not in a clean way. I do not have to go on a computer to see porn. Anyone can go to a church, or almost anywhere, and see it. The woman was his daughter showing most of it all. It sort of reminds me of one of the larger churches that I had gone to. One of the so-called preachers' wives would wear mini-skirts. The top part that she wore was not lady-like. It looked as though she bought her clothes at a yard sale. Some people try to look like that, so people would feel sorry for them. We can go to church, or almost any store, or public place and see porn.

As we move on, Hitler would love to have all of the modern tools we have today. The new world leader will have it all, and he will take over before my life is over, I believe. Yes, I remember a realtor witch that clipped me for over $20,000. Then there was another man that had real estate that didn't pay me for all of the work I did. He was married several times and lived in a big brick house. He drove a white van and had several kids from different wives.

Yes, then the people who didn't or would not pay when I did work for them. It would sometimes be the older so-called ladies from some church. I remember one that had her doctor's degree ,I guess, but I think a college gave it to her. I had done some for her for after her husband died. Her son paid me fair when I did work for him, but she was a cheater. She was self-righteous to the bone. They were kicked out of a church, I guess, for cheating people. Now in our time, many just keep the thieves. Yes, many of the older so-called ladies keep their money right to the grave.

One younger woman witch that worked for a bank, among other places, was going from church to church after different men. She was never satisfied. After a few years, she had gained a lot of weight and was still chasing the last time I saw her. Her dad had plenty of money, and I think she wanted a lot of it, or she told me that. I knew her family and her mom passed on. I think that is when she started to go downhill. We must remember the love of money is the root of all evil.

CHAPTER 7
Amendment #2

Yes, one place that I used to visit once in a while had many witches in it. I remember when I told one of the witches about God's judgment coming. She told me that I was crazy, and it was because she never heard about the Bible where she came from. I guess she thought she didn't believe in God, but will one day.

It was that place where one girl worked there said she was smart. Well, she must not have been too smart, because she said that I had a gun in the building where she worked. She said she had her master's degree. Whoo. I remember at the same time the children from all the public schools coming there. It was in the morning as I sat in there. They were teaching them all witchcraft. It was the same time that the witch that was ahead of the master's degree girl witch signed a paper to keep me out of the place. Anyone knows me knows I wouldn't carry a gun in there. One reason is they don't have enough money for me to rob the place.

It reminded me of the church that had been robbed of about $50,000. Most of it was probably checks anyway. Later on, some people heard that I carried a gun, I guess, because of the witch. The rumor was that I had robbed the rich church because I had gone there sometimes. It seemed like they had a lot of perverts there. The so-called preacher even said use whatever Bible you have. They used several Bibles, and where it seems money to pay the high cost of so-called preachers. The churches in the area had a boycott.

Yes, we are living in the last days. Many of the places that we eat at have all kinds of sin in them. Yes, many of the Sodom type run them and work there. It is not only restaurants but many other businesses.

We live in a day when many people say there is no hell. The day I was saved, I knew that a hell was there. Jesus talked about it many times. It seems that most people that go to church will be there also.

Chapter 8
Chickens Come Home

Yes, all of the contractors that didn't pay me, one looked like a girl that I worked for. All his help was on dope. Many were like that even in the market places, the ones that wore white shirts and nice clothes. Yes, I remember the greatest witch that I had ever met said she could say anything she wanted. Now the chickens have come home to roost, and her face is full of crap. It is like many others that thought they would get by, but no. It is like the greatest witch in the land is breaking most laws, lying, etc.

Yes, the greatest witch in our land has allowed everything we say, or don't say, to be recorded. We are being watched and may be picked up or shot, any day. After the greatest witch I have ever met had me kicked out, they tapped my phone for five years. I found out that it is the rules they put in place. I knew it was tapped, so I started to scare them.

We have witches all across our land like that now. It is why we have bloodshed, and God hates it. The people that are supposed to protect some of us are not. They are breaking laws themselves and are having many problems themselves because of it. They are getting killed right and left, and a lot of it is because they let people ,like the greatest witch I ever met, get by with sin.

The chickens have come home to roost. The preacher who was against the witch was threatened, and many people are witches because the newspapers backed the witch. The chickens have come.

Yes, one of the witches was a so-called deacon who came to my house and used words on me because I wouldn't work for him for nothing. He was the Head Deacon of his church. He worked at an electric company. He came to my house one morning and used bad words on me. Well, I told him that the chickens would come to roost one day. Then one day they did, one of his friends was shot and killed one evening. Just guess who killed him? I knew the man, and it was about money, as usual.

Then there was the witch that was going to put the story about my books in the newspaper, but she was a lost soul and changed her mind. She was from the church on Seven Hills.

As I said before, the ones that are to protect us are not always true. I remember one that followed me to work about two miles for no reason. Then we wonder who to trust. They want to make them under one ruler. Many witches want to have guns to protect themselves, but do not want you to have one. Then if you have one, they want it registered. They can put anyone on a "no fly list" just so you can't have a gun. Yes, Jesus told the disciples to take swords with them, and that is the same as two guns today.

Chapter 9
Vacation Time

Yes, I remember the so-called preacher as he took his family on a vacation. Yes, he had broken the law big time, and some of the others. He went to see a lawyer just in case they got sued. I, of course, have a better plan. I will just tell everyone the truth in words instead of trying to sue you people with deep pockets. This way I will win. I knew the lawyer and his family, and I had dinner with them at one time. One of them told me about the high middle-class yuppies. It is one reason God is not blessing the church, and his hand is not protecting it, nor our land.

It is sort of like the people of whom are to protect us. We all know that most of the time they do their job right, but sometimes they break the laws themselves. It is like one town where they pull someone over for no reason. I saw it happen. Then, when a poor person calls them, they do not respond, but if a rich man calls; they run. It is like the man that ran a stop sign in a small town, the man called in; they didn't even give him a ticket. The same town someone got pulled over, it cost over $80. It is why we see their car windows broke out, and many of them being killed, because God's hand is not protecting our land anymore. I remember seeing the car windows broke, so they put a fence up.

Yes, many witches, the one that drove a truck and worked for the utilities, was a drunkard and living with his third harlot. He and his new gal was a joke, and the law didn't bother him because he had little money. They had cheated me like the so-called Deacon that wanted me to work for them.

CHAPTER 10
Lunch Time

Yes, witches are everywhere it seems. It is like a restaurant that I would go to sometimes, the people that worked there, sort of looked like the hog that I used to see as a young man. They had rings in their nose, in their eyebrows, lips, tongue, tattoos all over them. They would curse each other out like a bunch of animals. The building looked clean on the outside, and most of it looked clean on the inside, I guess. As I took a closer look, I just couldn't eat there anymore.

The place was just like a bunch of animals. Some were having babies by any dog that came around. They were switching. It sort of reminded me of the greatest witches workplace. It all looked good on the outside and even on the inside, until you looked at what they were really doing. Many people there were from the church on Seven Hills. Most of the people were rude, and lost souls. I think one Spanish lady was saved. The rest, for the most part, were harlots, drunkards, and druggies, the Sodom type. It seemed like the worse a person looked the more they liked them. They, for the most part, had tattoos all over them, rings coming out of their noses, like a pig. Rings in their tongue, eyebrows, lips, big earrings in their ears, even the so-called men. Many of them were boasting they were on drugs.

The so-called restaurant was sort of like a rat hole. The rat hole is a place where an old lady owns. She has several of them. She lets people, old folks only, live there for taxpayer money. She bought them for hardly nothing and makes a lot. They have a person who fixes their meals, which isn't much, and they have tiny bedrooms as small as a bathroom. I knew of a lady who was staying there and was in a mental state. She said one of her relatives took all her money and put her in there. As I looked at the rat hole, the more I was concerned. The owner didn't like it and told me I wasn't allowed there anymore. That was okay with me, because I couldn't really do much. The witch tried to get me in a snare by calling me and asking me to come down there. The one that had mental problems called back and was crying, because she didn't have any friends and wanted me to come, but I didn't. One lady was visiting her, trying to help her, and she worked for a Socialist outfit. It was run by a witch also, although they used religion. He may have been related to one of the so-called preachers, who had a Doctor's degree. I remember, because the man had a so-called Doctor's degree himself. The place he was took care of poor people, it used to be independent, but went socialism for more money. He would be on the radio, etc., raising a whole lot of money. I think he may have given me a book he wrote. It was silly. I gave it away. Much can be said, because the money lover wrote me a few days later asking for money, after the cult's so-called preacher talked to him.

Yes, they are some of the middle-class that are being done away, as we live, because of their sin, and abuse. Yes, the witches go around parking lots and write down license plate letters etc, at churches and gun shows. We are all sinners, but some think that they are not. They take the money from them and then abuse them.

Yes, the greatest witch thought she got away with it by lying, and acting like she was a God. She is not, for the chickens have come home to roost.

We should be able to go around anywhere without people bothering us, but we can't it seems. People are writing books about witchcraft, and many are practicing it. Many movies have it in them, moving objects. We are living in the last days and the world is getting ready for the world government. It is getting closer every day.

Many of the good churches have turned into cults, and have people confused. The world is looking for a new world leader, and he will be the beast. The whole world will follow him, and God will let him bring fire out of the sky. He will say that he is God. All of this could take place almost any day, as people are blinded.

As this is happening right before our eyes, the world will have a cashless society. A few people want to control everything, and people that want the truth to be known. They are even using people who are to be caring of the law. Many of them are being shot as anarchy is taking over. The greatest witch I ever met is involved in the scheme. Her and her friend will have the mark of the beast, for they are lost souls.

ABOUT THE AUTHOR

I have written several books. This one is more political, and I talk about things that have happened in my life. It is also scary because they have changed my life, and your perhaps. I have written this book to help people understand more about the days we are living in. I believe we are seeing witchcraft more every day, and that is a sign of the last days. I am a child of God, and believe the rapture is coming soon, in God's time.

About the Book

This book is about many people, and many things that have happened in my life. The book is about how many people who have stolen from me, and lied for money. It is about witches. I call them that for the evil things they have done, and tried to ruin my life, because of their power, or position. It will open the eyes of many people. It is about some of the wickedness that is going on all across our land. It is sad in a way. Only God's people know the end is near, and even for our country.

www.ingramcontent.com/pod-product-compliance
Lightning Source LLC
LaVergne TN
LVHW012059070526
838200LV00070BA/3405